RELIGIONS OF HUMANITY

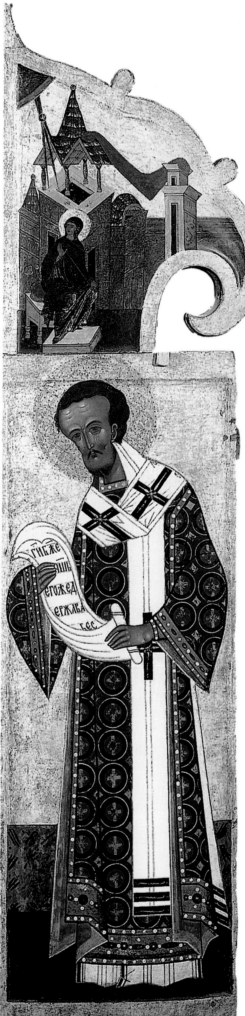

Chelsea House Publishers
1974 Sproul Road, Suite 400
Broomall, PA 19008

The Chelsea House
world wide web address is
www.chelseahouse.com

English-language edition
© 2002 by Chelsea House
Publishers, a subsidiary
of Haights Cross
Communications
All rights reserved.

First Printing

1 3 5 7 9 6 4 2

Left: Central part of the royal door painted in 1475 for the iconostasis of Saint Nicholas church in the monastery of Gostinopol'e at Novgorod, Russia, nowadays in Tret'jakov Gallery, Moscow. The upper section shows the angel's Annunciation to Mary, the lower section two bishops. In Orthodox churches, the iconostasis separates the nave, where the faithful gather, from the "sanctuary," where the altar is located. It is a partition entirely covered with icons depicting Christ, saints, prophets, and liturgical feasts. Three doors open in it: one at the center, also known as "royal door," and two at the sides.

Facing page: A young woman praying in a church in Belgrade, Serbia, in 1998. The iconostasis is clearly visible, the Annunciation painted on its royal door.

Library of Congress Cataloging-in-
Publication Data Applied For
ISBN: 0-7910-6628-2

© 2001 by
Editoriale Jaca Book spa, Milan
All rights reserved.
Originally published by
Editoriale Jaca Book, Milan, Italy

Design
Jaca Book

Original French text by
Olivier Clément

OLIVIER CLÉMENT

THE CHURCH OF
ORTHODOXY

CHELSEA HOUSE PUBLISHERS
PHILADELPHIA

CONTENTS

Construction of the great church dedicated to Saint Sava, the patron of Serbia, in the center of Belgrade at the end of the 1980's. The majesty of the construction in reinforced concrete follows traditional architectural styles.

INTRODUCTION

The Orthodox Church, along with Roman Catholicism and Protestant denominations, is one of the three important expressions of Christianity. Its heritage of holiness and beauty, and of spiritual intelligence, is considerable. Like Catholicism, Orthodoxy is rooted in original Christianity and is considered to have been created by God with the Incarnation and the Pentecost. It was primarily developed in the Middle East and in Eastern and Southeastern Europe: this geographical area is often called the "Christian Orient (or East)." Zealous missionaries then brought it to the North Pacific and to sub-Saharan Africa. But above all, Orthodoxy has developed a presence throughout the West due to the extensive economic and political migrations of the 20th century.

The separation between Eastern and Western Christians, never completed, was a long process that began with the split between Rome and Constantinople in 1054 and lasted until the 1870 proclamation of papal infallibility, which was unacceptable to the Orthodox. This break was, and still is, the result of cultural and political issues, as well as partially theological differences about the Pope's primacy. These two different outlooks were complementary during the first millennium and could become so again. This may be a challenge for the future of Christianity.

The faithful entering the Saint Sergius Trinity monastery at Sergijev Posad, Russia, for a liturgical service. The monastery, rich with history, is frequented often by the people of Moscow.

ORTHODOXY AS THE MAJOR RELIGION: GREECE

From the 15th century to the beginning of the 19th, Greece was absorbed by the Muslim Ottoman Empire, and it was the Greek church which maintained the country's language and culture (through "secret schools"). This is why, for Greeks, their country and church are inextricably linked. The faith is less important than a strong sense of membership. The Orthodox Church provides the framework for daily life in Greece. Time is measured by liturgical holidays. Rather than celebrating birthdays, for example, Greeks celebrate their saint days—the day carrying their first name—because the saint's name links them directly to the communion of the saints. For Theophany on January 6, the holiday celebrating Christ's baptism in the Jordan River, priests, accompanied by a crowd, bless the sea and throw a cross in the water. The young people then must brave the freezing water to retrieve it. The Russians have a similar tradition breaking the ice on the rivers.

1

Easter is the holiest time of the year: "Christ is risen from the dead!". Each family gathers for a special meal of a lamb raised from birth. Transfiguration, August 6, is the holiday to bless the fruits of the summer. The country is scattered with sanctuaries for pilgrimages, and monasteries are often surrounded by Eden-like gardens. Rural areas are strewn with chapels, each maintained by a family. Many pre-Christian sacred places are venerated with different names: springs, consecrated to the Mother of God, "spring of life"; mountains have their own chapel to the Prophet Elijah (on Mount Athos, it is a chapel to the Transfiguration). On these festivities, Greek enjoy popular dancing. The Church and the State are not separate. Sometimes conflicts between the Church and the State are pacified by monks from Athos, for instance sending a venerated icon to Athens, an icon brought by some monks and which is solemnly received by members of the government.

This situation favors tendencies toward religious nationalism—indeed, demagogy. But it also favors the interweaving of daily life and culture with communitarian and liturgical life (a major poet, Elytis, used the image of a Christian mountain and a pagan mountain in his significant work, "Athos and Pindus," where Athos, a mountain with connections to the 12th century hesychaste spiritual Orthodox movement, represents the Christian mountain, and Pindus, a mountain consecrated to Apollo and the muses, represents the pagan mountain).

1. The uneven mountainous terrain and the rugged landscape of Mount Athos, Greece, the Holy Mountain of Orthodoxy. Today Mount Athos is covered with monasteries. It has been the place of choice for hermits and ascetics since ancient times.
2. The Greek monastery of Amorgós. Leaning up against the rocks and almost rooted in the sea, it exemplifies very well the ties of local Orthodoxy to the Greek land.
3. A Greek Orthodox priest blesses the waters and the boats anchored in port.
4. An Orthodox wedding, which typically includes a ritual coronation. This coronation signifies that the bride and groom are sovereigns over each other and that true love deserves the crown of martyrdom, since it requires the death of one's egoism.

THE SPREAD OF ORTHODOXY

1. *A 12th century crater, a bowl or vase used to hold holy water, from the cathedral of Saint Sophia in Novgorod, is today housed in that city's museum.*

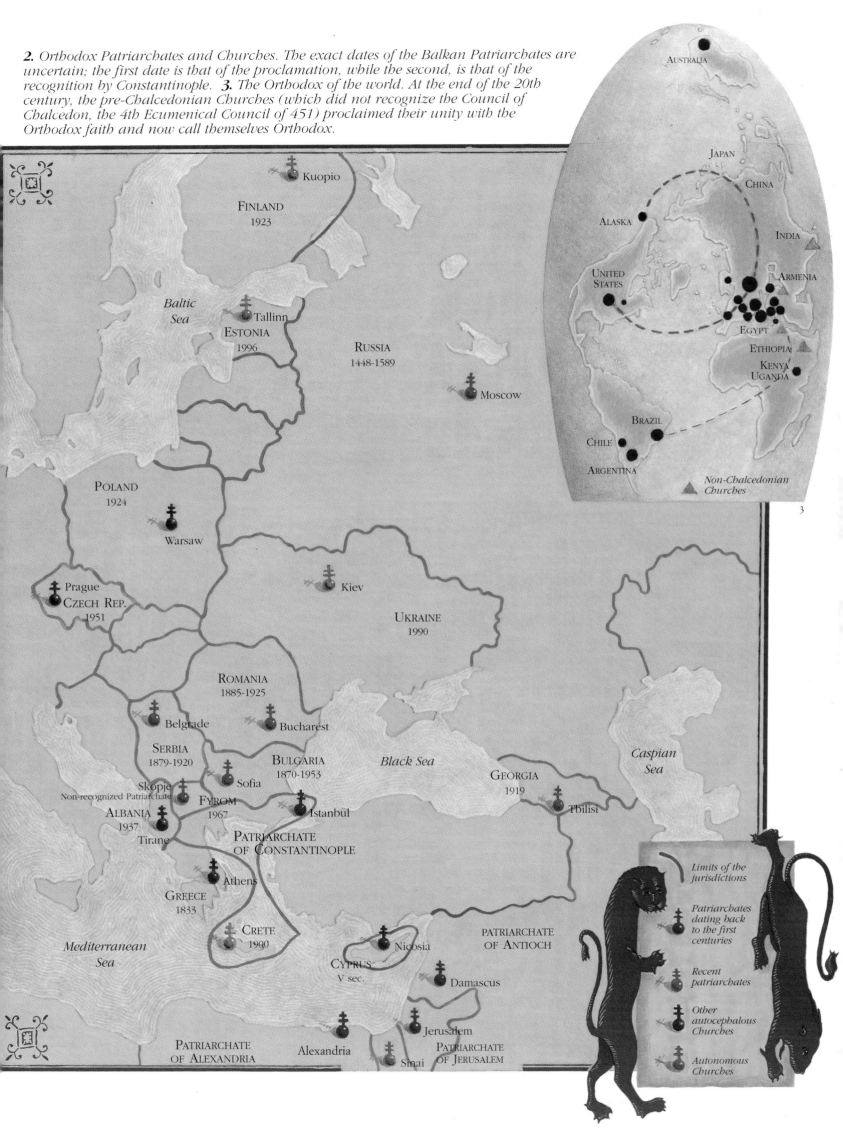

2. *Orthodox Patriarchates and Churches. The exact dates of the Balkan Patriarchates are uncertain; the first date is that of the proclamation, while the second, is that of the recognition by Constantinople.* **3.** *The Orthodox of the world. At the end of the 20th century, the pre-Chalcedonian Churches (which did not recognize the Council of Chalcedon, the 4th Ecumenical Council of 451) proclaimed their unity with the Orthodox faith and now call themselves Orthodox.*

AUSTRALIA

JAPAN

CHINA

ALASKA

INDIA

UNITED STATES

ARMENIA

EGYPT

ETHIOPIA

KENYA
UGANDA

BRAZIL

CHILE

ARGENTINA

Non-Chalcedonian Churches

3

Kuopio

FINLAND
1923

Baltic Sea

Tallinn

ESTONIA
1996

RUSSIA
1448-1589

Moscow

POLAND
1924

Warsaw

Prague
CZECH REP.
1951

Kiev

UKRAINE
1990

ROMANIA
1885-1925

Belgrade

Bucharest

SERBIA
1879-1920

BULGARIA
1870-1953

Black Sea

GEORGIA
1919

Caspian Sea

Skopje
Non-recognized Patriarchate

Sofia

Tbilisi

ALBANIA
1937

FYROM
1967

Istanbul

Tirane

PATRIARCHATE
OF CONSTANTINOPLE

Athens

GREECE
1833

CRETE
1900

Nicosia

PATRIARCHATE
OF ANTIOCH

Mediterranean Sea

CYPRUS
V sec.

Damascus

Jerusalem

PATRIARCHATE
OF ALEXANDRIA

Alexandria

PATRIARCHATE
OF JERUSALEM

Sinai

Limits of the jurisdictions

Patriarchates dating back to the first centuries

Recent patriarchates

Other autocephalous Churches

Autonomous Churches

ORTHODOXY IN THE MINORITY: DIASPORA, THE FRENCH EXAMPLE

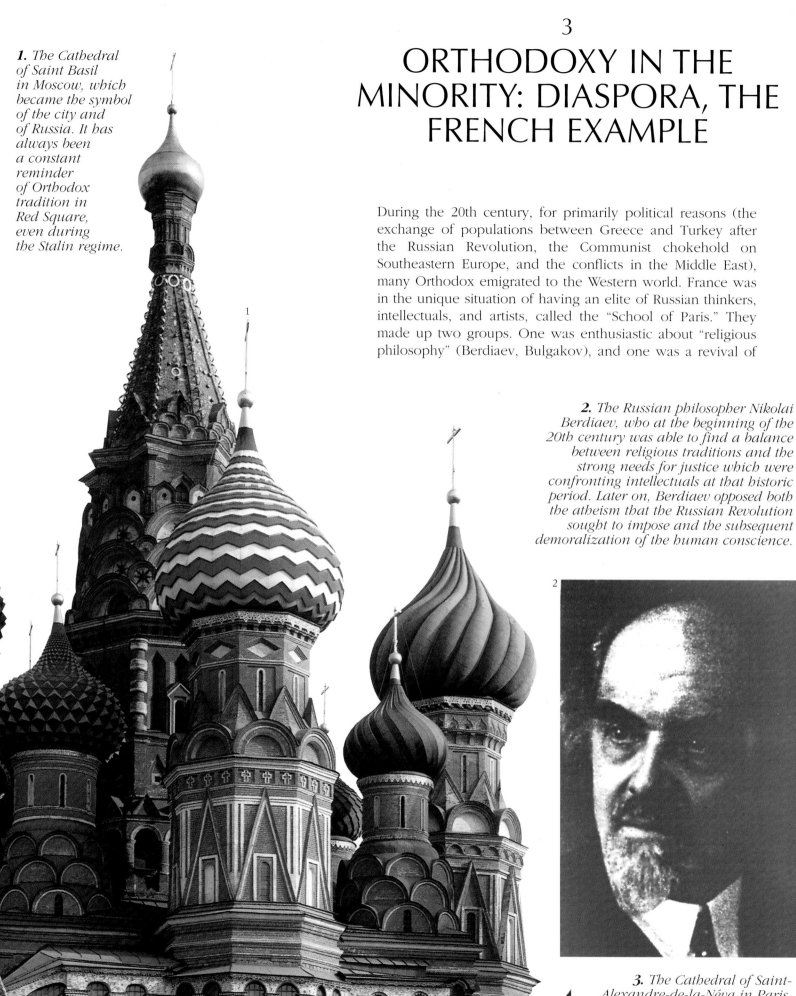

1. *The Cathedral of Saint Basil in Moscow, which became the symbol of the city and of Russia. It has always been a constant reminder of Orthodox tradition in Red Square, even during the Stalin regime.*

During the 20th century, for primarily political reasons (the exchange of populations between Greece and Turkey after the Russian Revolution, the Communist chokehold on Southeastern Europe, and the conflicts in the Middle East), many Orthodox emigrated to the Western world. France was in the unique situation of having an elite of Russian thinkers, intellectuals, and artists, called the "School of Paris." They made up two groups. One was enthusiastic about "religious philosophy" (Berdiaev, Bulgakov), and one was a revival of

2. *The Russian philosopher Nikolai Berdiaev, who at the beginning of the 20th century was able to find a balance between religious traditions and the strong needs for justice which were confronting intellectuals at that historic period. Later on, Berdiaev opposed both the atheism that the Russian Revolution sought to impose and the subsequent demoralization of the human conscience.*

3. *The Cathedral of Saint-Alexandre-de-la-Néva in Paris, built in 1861. Formerly it was the church of an embassy.*

followers of Gregory Palamas, a 13th century monk. This second group (Florovskii, Losskii, Meyendorff) also focused on the study of the doctrine of the Fathers of the Church. Two centers of learning and thought opened: the Saint-Serge Theological Institute in Paris, and the Saint Vladimir Seminary near New York (to which the Greek-influenced Holy Cross Theological School was added in Boston).

The parishes played an essential social and spiritual role in the spread of this new Orthodoxy. They constituted meeting places for immigrants from different nations and their families. But the rise of Orthodox parishes in the West brought about a change to the vernacular—parishes began conducting services in their local languages: French, English, Dutch. In addition, books about Orthodoxy and spirituality were published in these languages. *Philokalia* (literally, "Love of Beauty"), an anthology of spiritual texts, was translated into Italian, French and English. Necessary liturgical reforms began to take hold. This, in turn, little by little, brought about an awareness of the universality of Orthodoxy, within a context of personal experience and dialogue.

This gave an important ecumenical role to the Diaspora. Nowadays "The Prayer of Jesus" and, particularly, the icon itself, have become widespread far beyond the limits of Orthodoxy. Divided into "jurisdictions" depending on the traditional Churches, the Diaspora swings between nationalistic conservatism and the still timid development of local Churches. A unification effort in France resulted in the creation of an Assembly of Bishops, led by a representative of Constantinople. But the autocephalous (self-governing) Church established by Moscow in North America was not recognized by Constantinople, and in Canada and the United States Orthodoxy remains divided.

4. *From Paris to America. The Orthodox emigration from Russia and Eastern Europe across the Atlantic Ocean established important Orthodox communities even in the United States.*

3

4

HISTORY AS PROPHECY, MISFORTUNE AND FUNDAMENTALISM

1. The excommunication of the Patriarch Michael of Constantinople in 1054 by Pope Leo IX is illustrated in this Greek manuscript kept in Palermo, Italy. In 1965 the anathemas that the two Churches had exchanged for centuries were lifted by Pope Paul VI and Patriarch Athenagoras.
2. During the Fourth Crusade, Constantinople was besieged, as we see in this Spanish manuscript from the 13th century. The sack of the city and sacrilegious acts against sacred sites deepened the wounds of separation between Eastern and Western Christians.

1

2

The story of Orthodoxy is one of deaths and resurrections. After the golden age of the Fathers of the Church and of Byzantine theology, most Orthodox countries (except Russia) were subjugated to Islam and crippled by Catholic proselytization and Uniatism. Orthodoxy was reduced to a rural monastic culture. During the 18th century, the Russian government, in an attempt to modernize itself, attempted to control the Church: Peter the Great suppressed the Patriarchate of Moscow and replaced it with a Synod ruled by a high-level civil functionary. At the same time, the sultans scoffed at the Patriarchate of Constantinople. The Church's resurrection came at the end of the century with a powerful spiritual revival ("The Prayer of Jesus," the publication of a large anthology of mystical theology entitled *Philokalia*, and the development of a charismatic "paternity"). This revival worked its way from Moldavia to Mount Athos in Greece, and Russia, following the North-South axis of Orthodox unity.

In the 19th century, monasticism was revived by a group of Russian spiritual leaders (called *startsy*). The interest in them expressed by major writers and philosophers further amplified the revival in Russia. A great writer, Dostoevski, took a modern look at theology through his explorations of the abyss of the soul where he finds Christ as victorious over death and Hell. Because of Dostoevski's writings, the prophecy of Russian "religious philosophy" gained momentum and spread. But this revival, which culminated in the Moscow Council of 1917-1918, was crushed by the Bolshevik Revolution. Then came the time of martyrs—and of compromise. Orthodoxy revived once again after the collapse of Communism, but the invasion of American culture, the aggression of sects, and the blunders of other Christian groups contributed to a fundamentalist, anti-Western movement that rejected both ecumenism and liturgical reforms. Living thought and spirituality were rejected and the Church, unable to handle and understand modernity and the cultural changes, demanded protection from the government and, in turn, allowed itself to become politicized.

5. The Russian Patriarch under house arrest. The drawing is symbolic of the violent politics of Bolshevism with regard to the Orthodox Church, which witnessed destructions, sacks, executions and restrictions of liberty.

3. The refectory of the monastery of Dionysiou, Mount Athos, Greece, where Saint Nikodemos the Athonite (1749-1809) took his vows. Nicolas Kallivurtsis, his given name in life, along with Makarios Notaras, were responsible for compiling the "Philokalia," the text that has constituted since that time an inexhaustible fountain of spiritual teachings.

4. A graphic sketch of the Russian author Dostoevskii taken from an intense portrait by the German painter Max Beckmann.

THEOLOGICAL FOUNDATIONS

God, who revealed himself through the depth of the cosmos and through a People and His Law, entirely manifests himself in the *Divine-humanity* of Christ. Absolute personal existence, and therefore in communion, Christ, as human being at his maximum, is a universal existence. He carries all of humanity within Him. He did not create evil, but He becomes incarnate to fight evil and give people, become again *created-creators*, the way to resurrection.

The "communion of saints," that is of the living, is the image and prolonging of divine existence itself. Jesus reveals that the divine abyss (about which we can only speak in the "apophatic" non-language, tending to the silence of the adoration) is, in reality, a paternal abyss, an abyss of love and liberty from which, through the Son, the Holy Spirit, the "giver of life," beams forth. God is so truly *one* that He carries within Him, without separation, the mystery of the *other*. God is Trinity—absolute unity and absolute diversity at once.

God is Secret and Love, totally unknowable but totally accessible. The divine energies—the light of the Transfiguration and, through the Eucharist, of the coming of Christ at the end of time—make of the universe a burning bush, which our own blindness still veils. Sanctity means to bring to the surface of history this secret incandescence to prepare for Kingdom Come.

Man is *image* of God, thus with his own freedom together with grace he can transform this image into a *resemblance*-participation; in this way he can avoid the conditionings of the world, or change them. He is called to an existence guided by the trinity—that is to say in Christ and in the power of the Holy Spirit, he is called to carry all of humanity within him while also respecting the differences between people.

"Divine" energies, the light of the Transfiguration, penetrate and carry all things, "nature" is only as real as penetrated by "grace." The universe is called upon to become eucharist.

In our time, the Russian "sophiology" thinkers Solov'ev, Florenskii and Bulgakov, have insisted on this omnipresence of Wisdom (*Sophia* in Greek), from the perspective of a divine humanism capable of taking on both Eastern divinity and Western humanism, as Solov'ev puts it.

1. Reflection on the reality of the incarnation may be considered as the true genius of Orthodoxy. This icon, known as the Virgin of Vladimir is also called the Icon of the Incarnation or of Tenderness (11th-12th century, Tret'jakov Gallery, Moscow).
The human aspect is expressed with moving participation and the divine aspect is present in the serious and consoling attitude of the Child.

2. Christ's descent to the Hell, fresco in the ancient church of the Holy Savior in Chora, today the Kariye Museum, Istanbul. This fresco shows the vigor with which Jesus removed Adam and Eve—and with them all of humanity—from the grave. He towers above the demolished doors of the Hell to bring Adam and Eve to a resurrection with Him.
3. The famous icon of the Trinity painted by Andrei Rublev between 1425 and 1427 for the Saint Sergius Trinity monastery at Sergijev Posad, Russia. Today it is kept in the Tret'jakov Gallery, Moscow.

THE CHURCH AS MYSTERY AND MISERY

These theological foundations are part of the Orthodox concept of the Church: Body of Christ, Temple of the Holy Spirit, House of the Father. The Church is a communion of faith and love because it is, first and foremost, made up of eucharistic communities. Permanent communion of these is assured by the presence among them of primates (important Church leaders) charged with encircling life and love: metropolites for regions, patriarchs for larger areas or different countries, finally, primacy of honor and service of the Ecumenical Patriarch of Constantinople ever since the separation of Eastern and Western Christians.

All ecclesiastical processes must have a synodal aspect.

Faith was, therefore, preserved during the first millennium by "ecumenical councils" (that is, held within the setting of the Roman Eastern Empire, which defined itself Christian and universal, thus ecumenical), which first specified the different aspects of Christ. Faith was also preserved by regional councils finally recognized by all of Orthodoxy: in the 14th century, on how the essence and energies in God are distinguished yet united; in the 17th century, to situate Orthodoxy between Rome and the Reformation; and in the 19th century, to condemn religious nationalism. In our time, the primates of autocephalous Churches gather in pan-Orthodox conferences and solemn assemblies in a conciliar perspective.

1. Embroidery from the last quarter of the 15th century originally from Moldavia. It depicts the communion of the Apostles. It was used during Mass to cover the chalice until the recitation of the Creed. These types of images are called "anamneses," which in Greek means memory, and differ from other representations of the Last Supper because they refer directly to the Eucharist; in fact, Jesus in the role of a priest distributes communion to the group of apostles.
Beginning in the 11th century, in the apsidal basins of Byzantine churches, Christ may be represented as a priest who gives communion to his apostles in the form of bread and wine. It is the expression of a liturgy that is carried out eternally in Heaven, and acts as role model for the earthly liturgy of the Eucharistic rite.

Still, all of this ecclesiastical development was compromised by the burden of history. Nationalism from the Balkan nations and Russia transformed the interdependence of autocephalous Churches into juxtaposed independences. The Church had difficulty reconciling this new freedom with the fact that it wanted the government's protection. Bishops form an oligarchy which is entered by co-optation; the Patriarch, who in Russia condemns all change and reform, is an absolute monarch. The Ecumenical Patriarchate of Constantinople, weakened by history with the advent of Balkan autocephalous Churches and the exchange of populations between Greece and Turkey, has difficulty playing its role of initiator, go-between, and coordinator.

2. View of the cathedral of the monastery of the Savior on the Miroža in Pskov, Northern Russia. This is one of the great places of artistic and religious expression dating back to the Middle Ages.
3. In 1989 the Berlin Wall had fallen and in Russia the Soviet regime was about to crumble. Here we see Soviet Premier Gorbachev and Alexis II, the new Patriarch of the Russian Orthodox Church. The Orthodox Church was preparing to begin new relations with the changing political powers (June, 1990).

3

THE LITURGY, "HEAVEN ON EARTH"

1. A monk from Mount Athos plays the "semantron," a wooden percussion instrument used to summon the faithful to liturgical services.
2. One of the icons representing a feast day found in the cathedral of the Trinity in Saint Sergius Trinity monastery at Sergijev Posad, Russia. In this depiction of the Last Supper the artist from the Rublev school has been able to express all of the drama of the moment. The piece is dominated by the gesture of Judas, who leaning over his plate, reveals himself as the traitor in front of the knowing gaze of Jesus.

It is first and foremost through liturgy that an Orthodox demonstrates his membership in the Church. Surrounding the mystery of mysteries—the Eucharist, in which all is done by the Holy Spirit at the request of the priest and the people—is an ample hymnography that inserts Biblical readings into a doctrinal and spiritual commentary. Thus, the theology of the Fathers of the Church and Councils transforms itself into poetry. Everything is chanted without any musical instruments, the music staying in the service of the word and using tones that bring to mind Greco-Roman antiquity and the Jewish religious service. The texts are woven with antinomies that reflect the fundamental antinomy between the inaccessible God and the Crucified. The liturgy is not only the proclamation of the word of God, but the anticipation of the Kingdom via the mediation of a peaceful and luminous beauty—as the Russian envoys to Constantinople said in the 10th century, "heaven on earth."

The ecstasy of the Resurrection lasts from Easter all through the feasts of the year, from Sunday, "first and eighth day" of the week, Eucharistic day, all through the week.

As soon as young children have been baptized/chrismated, they receive Communion. This event has been and continues to be very rare for adults. Liturgical languages, for example Slavonic in Russia, certainly steeped in poetry and mystery, have become incomprehensible to most. The most important prayers have, out of reverent fear, been transformed into "secret prayers." The congregants remain passive while the choir sings alone. Liturgy tends thus to become a sublime spectacle.

Today, the situation is improving almost spontaneously in many parishes that, particularly in Russia, are also developing an important social role in the community.

3. This thurible, a vessel used to burn incense during religious services, was a gift from a Tsarina to the cathedral of the Archangel of the Kremlin in Moscow. Incense is a vegetable resin which burns producing a perfume that from antiquity has had a ritualistic role: communication with the divine and a fragrance that surrounds the faithful.

4. June 12, 1988, outside the monastery of Saint Daniil, the new see of the Patriarchate of Moscow, we see the "Millennium" celebratory Mass presided over by the Russian Patriarch Pimen and concelebrated by other Orthodox patriarchs, in memory of the birth of the Christian Rus' in Kiev.

8
THE ICON

The veneration of saintly images was justified by the Seventh Ecumenical Council (Nicaea II, in 787). With the Incarnation which puts an end to the prohibitions of the Old Testament, God showed himself in the face of a man: "Whoever has seen me has seen the Father," said Jesus, in the Light of the Holy Spirit. The celebrated icon by Andrei Rublev (1360-1430) represents the movement of love that both unifies and diversifies the Trinity.

The icon appeared around the 6th century, when the symbol designating "from the outside" a person's holiness or sainthood appeared in the person's face. The icon makes a personal presence arise. There is no visible light source, nor shadow, nor "escape hatch": everything is lit up from the inside by God. The body is elongated, reaching toward the face, which in turn focuses on the gaze.

Starting in the 15th century, to demonstrate that the Christian temple was restarting and completing the temple of the Old Testament, a partition covered with icons, the *iconostasis*, both separated the sanctuary from the nave and bound them to each other as well.

The art of the icon, sober and measured, essentially theological, is a liturgical art that follows strict guidelines. This has not prevented artists from being creative, nor has it prevented real innovations, provided they stay in the realm of *divine-humanity*. After the iconoclastic crisis of the 8th and 9th centuries, icons, frescoes and mosaics became more and more hieratic—the focus was put on the divine. With the Renaissance in the 14th century, humanism was reaffirmed. During the modern era, artists created imposing masterpieces from Athos to Aleppo, reaching the apex of beauty and profundity of spirit in the frescoes of the Moldavian monasteries. After decadence in a later period, the art of the icon has been reborn again today, notably thanks to the "School of Paris" (Grigorij Krug and Leonid Uspenskij).

1. The great artist Theophanes the Greek depicted while painting an icon in the second half of the 1300's. Miniature from the 16th century, Library of the Academy of Sciences in Saint Petersburg, Russia.
2. Icon of the feast of Christmas painted in Novgorod, Russia during the 15th century and today housed in the Tret'jakov Gallery, Moscow. Various scenes are present at the same time: Mary reclining according to Orthodox tradition; the Child Jesus in the manger with the donkey and the ox (who represent the various peoples of the earth); the arrival of the Magi·whit their gifts; the announcement to the shepherds; in the foreground Saint Joseph and women bathing the Child Jesus; the star with three rays descending from above; and in the upper portion, three saints.

3. *Twentieth century icon by the painter Grigorij Krug executed for the Hermitage of the Holy Spirit in Le Mesnil Saint-Denis, France. It represents Saint Gregory the Iconographer, a saint and painter of icons, who in the 3rd century contributed to the conversion of Armenia.*

4. *A monk painting in one of the monasteries of Mount Athos, Greece. The tradition of the iconographers has never ceased to renew itself through the centuries among the Orthodox monks who live in the monasteries on the Athos peninsula.*
5. *An iconostasis, recently erected and painted in a small women's monastery not far from the famous Monastery of Kalenić, Serbia.*

MONASTICISM AND HESYCHASM

Monks are essentially the "avant-garde" of the Orthodox Church; they have always prevented it from merging with "this world." There is only one monastic order, with no other end than contemplation, but with plenty of room for monks to pursue various personal vocations: from being in the community to being hermits, wanderers, and feigning madness. The monastic republic of Mount Athos in Northern Greece, where monks gather from all around the Orthodox world, has experienced a renewed strength.

The monks are rarely priests but are sometimes spiritual fathers (*startsy* in Russian), who have received the "discernment of the spirits." For laypeople they are role models and guides.

The axis of Orthodox monasticism is the hesychast tradition (from the Greek, *hesychia*, meaning peace, calm and silence of the union with God). "Art of arts and science of sciences," hesychasm uses a method which incorporates psychosomatic aspects: hence, the invocation of Jesus' name using the rhythm of breathing, sometimes of heartbeat, to favor the union of the mind and the heart (seen as the most central core of the being, where the person gathers himself and goes beyond himself).

Hesychasm comprises, in general, three stages:

1. *Practice*, ascetic effort to liberate oneself from idolatrous passions and transform into virtue the energy that these passions use up. Virtues are divine-human; their synthesis, within Christ, is internal liberty and love.

2. *Physical theory*, contemplation of God's glory in people and things, vision of their spiritual essences rooted in the divine Word (*Logos*).

3. *Divine theory*, the embrace of the heart-spirit by the uncreated Light, which shines from the Father, through the Son, into the Holy Spirit. Man becomes light, while turning toward the light's inaccessible source. This is "deification—taking part in God's mercy and His resurrection to fight against evil.

3

1. Monks working in the fields of Mount Athos, Greece. Work, both agricultural and artistic, is part of the monastic program, as it is in many analogous Western Christian communities.
2. A monk from Mount Athos in contemplation in front of the sea. In the background is the monastery of Stavronikita. The transparent sea lapping against the shores of the Holy Mountain seems to remind the monk of his calling to be "transparent" to God's action for the sake of the world.

3. View of the monastic complex of Studenica, Serbia (12th-14th centuries) and of a portion of its Mother of God church. This is one of the most important Serbian monasteries, which gave a great push to architecture and painting and became the bridge between the Byzantine art of the Slavic world and the Romanesque art of Western Europe.
4. A monk lighting a candle illuminating an icon. This is a scene of daily devotion. All Christians are invited to face the spirituality of Orthodox monasticism, since it has always been seen by Eastern Christianity as the point of reference for everyone, since each one is destined to make room in his life for the concrete presence of God.

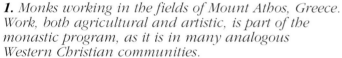

AN EXCERPTED WRITING BY FATHER SERGEI BULGAKOV ABOUT HIS CONVERSION

1. This 1889 painting by Mikhail Nesterov depicts a hermit, a figure often identified in Russian tradition with "starets," the spiritual father. Despite the solitude of this individual, the caring of souls was performed by men of great internal experience who also organized themselves in monastic communities.

The years were going by, and I could not find the strength to take the decisive step. [...] It remained this way until a strong hand raised me up. [...]

Autumn. A monastery hidden in the forest [...], I had taken advantage of the opportunity to come here, with the secret hope of encountering God. But all resolve abandoned me. I attended Vespers, unmoved and cold. After the service, I left the church practically running [...]. I rushed in anguish toward the monastery, blind to everything around me, and I came to my senses ... in a Starets' cell. I had been brought there—a miracle had happened to me [...]. At the sight of the prodigal Son, the Father hurried to meet him. I learned from him that all the sins of man amount to only a drop of water in the ocean of divine mercy. I left his cell pardoned, reconciled, trembling and crying. I felt as if I were being carried by wings into the church's enclosure [...]. I, too, had been affected by the Gospel that told of the pardon given to the woman who had greatly loved; and I was given a taste of the sainted Body and Blood of my Savior.

THE EVERLASTING LIGHT
translated from French, Lausanne, 1990, p. 25-26

Text written circa 1910. Bulgakov, who was forty years old at the time of its writing, was a deputy in the Russian Parliament. A former Marxist theoretician, he became increasingly attracted to Christianity.

2. Photograph of Sergei Bulgakov. The son of an Orthodox priest, he was born in Russia in 1871 and died in Paris in 1944. He was impressed by the rhythm of the liturgy and by a sense of the sacred land. At first he followed Marxism, but around 1910 he returned to his Christian faith. A scholar and a politician (deputy to the second Duma), he became a priest in 1918. Exiled in 1923, he settled in Paris where he founded the Saint-Serge Theological Institute.
He developed a powerful theological synthesis centered on the theme of Wisdom. Uncreated Wisdom is reflected in the face of God full of affection towards creation, and Created Wisdom is the transparency of creation in the presence of God. The total synthesis is realized in the Incarnation.
3. The Risen Christ appears to Mary Magdalen; 16th century icon from Crete, today in the Dubrovnik Museum, Croatia. Jesus appears alive to the woman who had been forgiven for having greatly loved, as we read in the passage quoted above.

GLOSSARY

words in CAPITALS are cross references

Antinomy: Orthodox theology and LITURGY often utilize antinomy. It poses two contradictory affirmations and says that they are both true, in a difference-identity. Thus, God is one and three, Christ is truly God and truly a man, and Glory and the Cross are inseparable.

Apophatism: with respect to God, there must be no assertion, image, quality or symbol that could be a limitation. God is always beyond, even beyond the concept of God. God cannot be described in human terms.

Asceticism: this word refers to exercise, interior fight—through spiritual fasting, celibacy, and keeping vigils (NEPSIS)—undertaken to reach a state of grace.

Athos: Mount Athos, also known as the "Holy Mountain," is a long peninsula located in Northern Greece. Its hills and mountains reach 2000 meters. Since the 10th-12th centuries, it is a federation of twenty sovereign monasteries, from all nationalities (there are also other less important communities and hermitages). When visiting Mount Athos, one discovers with amazement the beauty of nature, architecture, and frescoes, as well as the intensity of constant prayer, both liturgical and personal. All women are barred from Mount Athos, except for the Mother of God. For this reason, it is known as the "Garden of the Virgin." Today there are almost 2000 monks living there, many of whom are young and culturally sophisticated. A recent Church reform consolidated and developed community monasticism, to the detriment of "idiorhtymic" monasticism (that is, a way of life in which each monk follows "his own rhythm").

Autocephalous Churches: Orthodoxy is composed of independent self-governed national Churches, each of which elects its own primate—that is, "its own head." Autocephalous Churches are interdependent with one another. They must be recognized by others, and, most importantly, by the Ecumenical Patriarchate of Constantinople.

Baptism-Chrismation: these two sacraments, administered together through one rite, constitute the Christian initiation that permits an individual to take Communion. The baptism is a death-resurrection with Christ. The Chrismation is a personal Pentecost.

Burning Bush: the Angel of God appeared to Moses on Mount Horeb, in the form of a bush that was burning without being consumed or destroyed. This is a symbol with multiple meanings (Mary, the world in Christ…).

Council: assembly of bishops that specifies the rules of faith and the organization of the Church. It makes decisions unanimously, but it has to be "welcomed" by the community of the faithful. There are local, regional, and universal Councils.

It is important to distinguish between Councils convened for special events having to do with matters of a spiritual nature, and those convened regularly for administrative purposes (for example, those convened once or twice a year in a metropolitan see).

Diaspora: this word, taken from Jewish history, designates the modern dispersal of members of the Orthodox faith. How to organize the diaspora is a problem that remains unsolved within the Orthodox Church.

Easter: the "feast of feasts," that of the Resurrection: "Christ was resurrected from the dead, through death He defeated death, to those who are in tombs (that is, all men), He gave life."

Ecumenical: first meaning, universal, the inhabited Earth. From this meaning come the expressions "Ecumenical EMPIRE," "Ecumenical COUNCIL," and "Ecumenical Patriarchate." In modern times, this word designates the effort of Christians to regain their unity. The Orthodox Churches are, not without extreme difficulties, part of the Ecumenical Council of Churches, which brings together Protestants, Anglicans and Orthodox.

Empires: Orthodoxy has mostly existed in multinational Empires, whether they were inspired by Orthodoxy (Byzantine Empire, Russian Empire), tolerated it (Arab Empire, Ottoman Empire), or fought against it (Communist Empire).

Fathers of the Church: these are the major witnesses of faith—speaking theologically—who lived during the first millennium, particularly during the 4th century. If a saint, Maxime the Confessor, during the 7th century, was a simple monk, most of the Fathers were bishops commenting on Scripture to their people, often explaining liturgies, deepening faith through their writings, defending against the powers the independence of the Church, and developing ample social services for the benefit of the poor.

Gregory Palamas: this monk, a 14th-century theologian and bishop, in order to preserve the realism of "deification," distinguished between God's *inaccessible* essence and His *partecipable* energies. This was not a dichotomy, but rather an ANTINOMY, because "all of God is inaccessible and all of God is partecipable."

Iconoclast (from a Greek word meaning "image-destroyer"): supporter of **Iconoclasm,** a religious movement in the Byzantine EMPIRE that denied the holiness of sacred images; in the eighth and ninth centuries the use of such images was prohibited. Iconoclasm was condemned by the Council of Nicaea in 787.

Iconostasis (from a Greek word meaning "stand for image"): a partition with tiers of icons and three doors (the central one is called "royal door") separating the *bema* (the "sanctuary" where the altar is located and where only the priests are allowed for the celebration of the LITURGY) from the nave (where the faithful stay) in Orthodox churches. The rows of icons display, from top to bottom, the history of the salvation: the patriarchs, the prophets, the Church with the *Deesis* (a representation of Christ Judge flanked by the intercessory figures of the Mother of God at his right and John the Baptist at his left).

Kingdom: "of God," or, out of respect for the divine name, "of the skies." The experienced presence of God who, like in flashes, is anticipated in the mysteries and the mystical, in beauty and love, and who will manifest Himself in plentitude at the time of the ultimate transfiguration of the universe.

Liturgy: in a broad sense, the services and prayers. In a more specific sense, the eucharistic liturgy.

Nepsis: Vigil, vigilance. Night prayer. In a broad sense, it refers to "attention"—to Christ who comes through people and things.

Orthodoxy: refers to both correct doctrine and correct celebration.

Patriarch: title given to the bishop who heads an AUTOCEPHALOUS Church. The Patriarch is always seated "in his synod."

Philokalia: translated literally, this means "love of beauty." It is an Anthology of mystical theological texts. The Greek *Philokalia*, soon translated into SLAVONIC and then Russian, was published in Venice in 1782. In modern times, in Romania, Father Dumitru Staniloe edited an immense *Philokalia* with commentaries on current events.

Slavonic: the language created for the Slavs by the Greek brothers Cyril and Methodius in the ninth century, still used liturgically in the Russian Church.

Starets (plural **startsy**): "elder" in Russian, "geronda" in Greek. Every person, man or woman, no matter his/her place in the hierarchy, who, after a long ASCETICISM of deprivation, receives the donation of "discernment of spirits" or "cardiognosy" (reading of the hearts)—that is, the recognition of the other as a revelation.

Uniatism: in 1596 in Poland-Lithuania, in 1700 in Hungary, and in 1714 in the Middle East, the Catholic Church annexed ("united," from the Roman perspective) many Orthodox regions, allowing them to keep their rites but Romanizing their thoughts. After World War II, in eastern Europe, Stalin destroyed these communities. They were reconstructed after 1989, not without conflicts with the Orthodox there.

INDEX